PUPIL
WORKBOOK
YEAR 3

T0340559

Contents

Rocks, soils and fossils

Light and shadows

Friction and magnets

Movement and nutrition for the human body

Flowering plants and plant growth

Flowering plants life cycle

Rocks, soils and fossils

Lesson 1   How are rocks different and what rock is this?

Key vocabulary

crystal   material   property   rock

Activity 1: Comparing rocks

You will need
- two different types of rock
- a magnifier

Look at two different rocks. Compare them. Use a magnifier to look closely. If you do not have any rocks, use the images below.

rock 1

rock 2

Write short notes in the table. The words in the box may help you.

| rough | smooth | heavy | light | soft | hard |
| shiny | dull | crumbly | lines | holes | crystals |

	Rock 1	Rock 2
Colour		
Pattern		
Shape		
Soft/hard		
Texture		
Other features		

Activity 2: Drawing and labelling rocks

Choose three rocks. Observe them closely using a magnifier.

Draw each rock. Label each drawing with the rock's properties.

The words in the box on page 2 may help you.

Rock 1	Rock 2	Rock 3
Type: _____	**Type:** _____	**Type:** _____

Write in each box which types of rock you have drawn. Use the photographs and information below and on page 4 to help you. (Your rocks may not be the same colours as the ones shown here.)

pumice

Pumice is a very light rock. It has lots of small holes. It is white, grey or light brown and is rough to touch.

chalk

Chalk is a very soft, white or light grey rock. It is made from the shells of very small sea creatures. It is smooth and can be easily scratched.

granite

Granite is one of the hardest rocks. It is usually grey or pink. It is made up of **crystals**, which you can often see on the rough surface.

slate

Slate is fine grained and smooth, and is formed in thin, flat layers. It is usually grey, but can be other colours.

marble

Marble is a smooth rock. It comes in a range of colours including white, grey, pink and green. It feels cool to touch.

sandstone

Sandstone comes in a wide range of colours. It is made from sand, has a rough surface and is softer than granite or marble.

> **Compare your labelled drawings with your partner's drawings. How are they similar? How are they different?**

Choose two of your rocks or two from the pictures above. Write how they are similar and different to each other below.

_____

_____

_____

Key learning

In this lesson I have learnt that: **Rocks** are part of the Earth's surface. They are natural **materials** made of lots of tiny pieces that stick together. They are found in many places, for example in the soil or on the beach. Different types of rock have different **properties**. They might be shiny, rough or smooth, for example. We can compare and group rocks by their properties.

Homework

Look for rocks at home or on the way to school. What different types of rock can you find? Write the name of one type of rock you find. List the properties.

Lesson 2 What are rocks used for?

Key vocabulary

absorb/absorbent	durable	property	waterproof
comparative test enquiry	hardness	rock	weathering

Activity 1: Rocks all around us

Look at the pictures and discuss the questions with a partner or as a class.

Why was rock used to make these objects?

What properties do the rocks need to have? Why?

Activity 2: Weathering

Choose one of these three photographs.

Explain what you think has been done to the rocks to change the way they look.

_____

_____

_____

Activity 3: Which rock is best for a statue?

Imagine you are a stonemason (a person who shapes rock to make buildings or sculptures). You are going to make a statue. The statue will be placed outside. You need to choose the best type of rock.

You are going to carry out **comparative test enquiries** to test two properties:

- absorbency (whether the rock takes in water)
- durability (whether the rock is hard to scratch).

Test 1: Which rocks absorb water?

Put one drop of water on each rock. Observe carefully.

Is the water absorbed? How do you know? How long does it take?

Record your results in the table.

> **You will need**
> - six types of rock including marble and sandstone
> - water
> - water droppers

Name of rock	Does it absorb one drop of water?		How long does it take for one drop of water to be absorbed?		
	YES	NO	1 minute	2 minutes	3 minutes
Marble					
Sandstone					

Which rocks absorbed water fastest? _____

Did any rocks not absorb water? _____

Why would absorbency affect a statue? _____

_____

Test 2: Which rocks can be scratched easily?

Try to scratch each rock. Use your fingernail, a coin, a nail and a piece of hard rock.

Record your results in the table. One has been done for you.

Name of rock	Can the rock be scratched using ...			
	a fingernail?	a coin?	a nail?	another rock?
Marble	no	no	yes	no
Sandstone				

Which rocks were easiest to scratch? _____

Which rocks were hardest to scratch? _____

Why is a rock that cannot be scratched better for a statue? _____

_____

Think about what you learnt from both of your comparative tests.

Overall, which of the six rocks would be best for a statue and why? _____

_____

Key learning

In this lesson I have learnt that: Different **rocks** have different **properties**. For example, **waterproof** or **absorbent**, **hard** or soft, **durable** or fragile. These properties are useful for different purposes. **Weathering** is when rocks get worn down or broken over time by the weather. Some properties mean rocks will be more affected by weathering.

Homework

Look for rocks that show evidence of weathering. Make notes about the signs of weathering, what the rock is being used for, and how weathering has changed the object over time.

Key vocabulary

erosion   material   organic   property   rock   soil   weathering

Activity 1: Rocks breaking down

Look at the pictures below. What do you think will happen to these rocks over a long time?

_____

_____

_____

Draw a circle around the types of rock that you think will break down most easily.

pumice

chalk

granite

slate

marble

sandstone

Why do you think those rocks would break down easily? _____

_____

_____

Activity 2: Comparing and identifying soils

For each sample, take a spoonful of soil. Put the soil on the palm of your hand.

Look at it closely using a magnifier. Try to roll and squash the soil.

Record your observations in the first three rows of the table.

You will need
- three soil samples
- a spoon
- a magnifier

	Sample 1	Sample 2	Sample 3
What does it feel like?			
Will it squash together to form a ball?			
What else do you notice?			
Type of soil?			
How do you know?			

Look at the photographs and descriptions on the next page.

Can you identify your three soils? Write the types in the table. Explain how you know.

clay soil

- feels lumpy and sticky if wet
- rock hard when dry
- dark colour

silty soil

- smooth and 'soapy' to the touch
- soft, fine texture
- light colour

chalky soil

- gritty
- usually stony
- light colour

sandy soil

- large pieces of sand
- gritty
- light colour

peat-free soil

- crumbles easily
- light texture
- contains lots of organic material
- dark colour

loamy soil

- not gritty or sticky
- even-sized pieces
- forms clumps
- medium to dark colour

Compare your three soil samples.

Similarities: _____

Differences: _____

What evidence have you seen that soils are different? _____

_____

Key learning

In this lesson I have learnt that: **Soil** is made from tiny pieces of **rock** and **organic material** (the remains of living things that have died). Rocks are broken down into small pieces over a very long time, due to **weathering** or water **erosion**. Different soils have different properties. The **properties** depend on how much organic material and which types of rock are in the soil.

Homework

Choose a plant, for example cactus or rose. Find out which type of soil is best for that plant.

Key vocabulary

absorb/absorbent   material   property   soil

comparative test enquiry organic   rock

Activity 1: Why does the soil become flooded?

Amara grows vegetables in her garden.
When it rains a lot, the garden floods.

> Could the type of soil be
> causing the problem?
> Discuss with a partner.

Activity 2: How fast does water drain through different soils?

You are going to carry out a **comparative test enquiry** to measure how fast water drains through different types of soil.

Think about how you will use the equipment and set up your enquiry.

Tick (✓) to show what you will change, what you will keep the same and what you will measure.

You will need

- three soil samples
- a spoon
- a transparent beaker
- a funnel
- a timer or stopwatch

	Change	Keep the same	Measure
Type of soil	☐	☐	☐
Amount of soil	☐	☐	☐
Amount of water	☐	☐	☐
Time	☐	☐	☐

Construct your results table. Use these column headings:

- Soil type
- Description of soil
- Time taken for water to drain through
- Other observations

Now carry out your enquiry. Record the results in your table.

Results table: how soils drain

What did you find out from your enquiry? _____

_____

What type of soil do you think Amara might have in her garden? _____

What type of soil would you recommend Amara use? _____

Explain why. Use evidence from your enquiry. _____

_____

Key learning

In this lesson I have learnt that: One of the **properties** of **soil** is how easily water passes through it. Some soils allow water to drain away easily. Some **absorb** water and hold onto it. Some soils have air in them, as well as **rock** and **organic material**. These air pockets can fill with water. Generally, the larger the air pockets, the quicker water drains away.

Homework

Look for fields or areas in a park that are flooded after rain. Does the water disappear quickly or slowly? What might be making it take longer to drain away? Take photos and write descriptions of what you see.

Key vocabulary

fossil   remains   rock   sediment

Activity 1: Fossil observations

You will need

- replica fossils (optional)
- a magnifier
- a ruler (optional)

Choose three fossils. Use the photographs below, or replica fossils if available.

Record your observations in the table.

Type of fossil			
Description			
Size			
Animal, plant or something else?			

Ammonite

Ammonites were marine creatures with a spiral-shaped shell. The fossilised remains of their shells are often found on beaches. They are around 65 million years old. One of the largest ever collected was over two metres wide.

Clam

Very similar to modern clams and oysters. Most lived in the sea. Sometimes you find them with two shells joined together, or just one shell. If you find them on land, the place that you are searching used to be under the sea.

Sea urchin

Sea urchins have a round shell covered in spines. A sea urchin's spines often fall off when they die.

Trilobite

Trilobites lived in large groups around 540 million years ago. They are some of the oldest fossils. There are lots of different types of Trilobites, for example with different shaped heads or tails.

Coral

Corals look like plants but are actually made up of tiny sea animals. Corals grow in warm, shallow seas. Coral fossils are around 400 million years old.

Plant remains

Many kinds of plants have been preserved in mud. You may see fossilised leaves, branches, bark or fir cones. Many of these remains date back hundreds of millions of years.

Dinosaur parts

Fossil remains of different kinds of dinosaurs – bones, teeth and footprints – can tell us a lot about where and how they lived. Dinosaurs lived on Earth from about 225 million to about 65 million years ago.

Activity 2: Whose remains are these?

Match each fossil to the correct living thing.

Activity 3: How did fossils form?

Read the information in Key learning below. In what order did these things happen?
Write numbers 1 – 4 to show the order.

☐ **Layers of sediment form on top of the remains over a very long time.**	☐ **When the living thing dies, its remains fall to the seabed.**
☐ **The pressure of the rock building up over time cause the remains to change.**	☐ **The plant or animal is alive.**

Key learning

In this lesson I have learnt that: Some **rocks** contain **fossils**. A fossil is evidence of a plant or animal from a long time ago. When the living thing died, layers of **sediment** (small pieces of rock) formed on top, burying the plant or animal. After a very long period of time, pressure of this sediment caused the **remains** to turn into a fossil.

Homework

Find a fun fact about fossils to share with the class. Maybe the biggest or oldest ever found.

Key vocabulary

fossil   palaeontologist

Activity 1: Who was Mary Anning?

Read the information and discuss the questions below with a partner.

Mary Anning was born in 1799. She lived in England, in a town called Lyme Regis.

Mary's family was very poor. Her father was a carpenter. He made extra money by finding and selling fossils. Mary helped him.

When Mary was 11, her father died. She continued to find and sell fossils.

In 1811, Mary found the skeleton of an ichthyosaurus. Scientists were very interested in the find.

Over the years, she made many other discoveries. She became an expert in fossils, and was famous for it.

Mary died when she was 47 years old.

Mary Anning

> Do you think Mary was a scientist?

> How do you think she became a fossil expert?

fossil of an ichthyosaurus

Activity 2: Researching Mary Anning

You will need

- appropriate texts or web-based information about Mary Anning

What would you like to know about Mary Anning's life? Write questions in the table.

Research Mary Anning's life. Write the answers to your questions if you can.

When in Mary's life?	Possible questions	Answers
Early life – as a child and young girl, before her father died		
As a young woman – after her father died and as she tried to make money for her family		
As a fossil expert and successful business woman		

How did you do your research? _____

_____

_____

Were any of your questions difficult to answer? Why? _____

_____

_____

_____

Do you think scientists today view Mary Anning differently from the scientists in her time? Why?

_____

_____

_____

What scientific skills did you use in this lesson? _____

_____

_____

_____

Key learning

In this lesson I have learnt that: Mary Anning was born in England in 1799. As a child, Mary started finding **fossils** and selling them. When she grew up, she became a fossil expert, using her observations to improve her and others' understanding of the natural world. She made lots of amazing discoveries and is one of the most famous **palaeontologists** in the world, though at the time many people did not think she was a 'serious' scientist.

Homework

Find out about Anjana Khatwa. How is she similar to Mary Anning? How is she different? Make some notes to share with the class.

Light and shadows

Lesson 1 — What do we need to see?

Key vocabulary

bright	dim	light source
dark	light	Sun

Activity 1: Identifying light sources

Look at the light sources on this page. What other light sources can you think of? Add examples to the table and choose whether they are natural or artificial.

Light source	Natural (✓)	Artificial (✓)

Choose one of the light sources. Write a sentence about what a light source is using your example.

_____

Activity 2: What can you see inside a dark tent?

Go somewhere very dark, for example a dark tent. What can you see and what can't you see?

_____

_____

Why do you think this is?

I think this is because _____

Activity 3: What objects can you see in dim light?

Place the objects inside the box and peep through the hole.

Which objects could you see?

The objects that were easier to see in **dim** light were:

_____

_____

_____

You will need

- cardboard box with peephole
- counters or pens/pencils
- coins
- pieces of foil
- buttons or stones

Circle the words that describe what these objects looked like:

light / bright coloured   **dull**   **shiny**   **dark coloured**

When we took the lid off the box it was easier to see the objects because _____

_____

_____

What two things do we need to be able to see?

1. _____

2. _____

Key learning

In this lesson I have learnt that: **Light** comes from **light sources**. The **Sun** is a source of natural light. Electric lights are sources of artificial light. **Darkness** is the absence of light. Nothing can be seen if there is no light. Objects are easier to see when there is more light.

Homework

What natural and artificial sources of light are there in your home and on your way to school? Make a list and discuss them with your classmates. Remember to notice if they are natural light sources or artificial light sources.

Lesson 2 — Which object is the most reflective?

Key vocabulary

light source   lux   reflect   reflective   sensor

Activity 1: Which object reflects the most light?

Plan an investigation of a selection of different objects to find out which object is the most reflective.

Draw a diagram with the arrows to show how you will do the investigation and how you will measure how reflective an object is.

Label the torch, object and light sensor.

You will need

- mirror
- torch
- data logger
- shiny and dull objects to test

What is the **light source** in your test? _____

What do you need to keep the same in your test to make it fair?

_____

_____

Complete your investigation and use the table to record your results.

Object	Amount of light reflected (lx)	Order (most to least reflective)

Which is the most reflective object?

_____

How did you know?

_____

_____

Choose the correct words below to complete the sentences:

sources   **shiny**   **dull**   **more**   **night**

_____ objects are easier to see than _____ objects when there is not much light.

Their surface reflects _____ of the light that shines on them from light _____ into our

eyes. This makes them reflective. Reflective materials can keep us safe at _____ .

Key learning

In this lesson I have learnt that: Some objects appear shiny as they **reflect** light very well from their surface. We say they are **reflective**. Mirrors are very reflective. Lots of light reflects (bounces off) the surface of a mirror. Scientists can use a light **sensor** on a data logger to measure light. Light is measured in **lux** (lx).

Homework

Can you find any objects at home, or when you are outside, that have reflective materials on them? What is the reflective material for?

Key vocabulary

light   opaque   translucent
light source   shadow   transparent

Activity 1: Identifying different materials

Discuss the meanings of the words to the right as a class. Use the words to label the picture with the type of material the girl is holding up.

- **opaque**
- **transparent**
- **translucent**

_____   _____   _____

Activity 2: How can you make the darkest shadow?

You are going to test materials to find out which makes the darkest shadow by holding them in front of a screen.

Which of the materials do you predict will make the darkest shadow?

_____

Why do you think it will make the darkest shadow?

_____

_____

You will need

- screen
- torch
- transparent, translucent and opaque materials to test

Which of the materials do you predict will not make a shadow? _____

Write why you think this is.

_____

_____

Record your observations in the table.

Material	What the shadow looks like	Order (darkest to lightest shadow)

Were your predictions correct? Explain why or why not.

_____

_____

Which material produced the darkest shadow?

_____

Which material produced no shadow?

_____

Activity 3: What did you find out?

Draw a diagram to show how you made a shadow.

Complete the sentence.

The darkest shadows are made by _____

materials because _____

_____

_____

_____

Match each word to the description of its shadow.

| Opaque | ● | ● | No shadow as it lets all the light through |

| Translucent | ● | ● | Dark shadow as it blocks all light |

| Transparent | ● | ● | Faint shadow as it blocks some of the light |

Key learning

In this lesson I have learnt that: **Shadows** are formed when **light** from a **light source** is blocked. **Transparent** materials are materials you can see through, like glass. **Opaque** materials are materials you cannot not see through, like card. **Translucent** materials are materials you can partly see through, like tracing paper. Opaque materials block all the light so objects made from opaque materials cast the darkest shadows.

Homework

Make shadows on a wall at home using a torch or light without anyone seeing the object you are holding. Can someone in your home guess what it is? Explain how you made the shadow.

Key vocabulary

opaque   shadow   sunlight   ultraviolet (UV)

Activity 1: My shadow

Make a shadow on the playground on a sunny morning. Draw a diagram of yourself and your shadow. Draw the position of the Sun.

How did you make a shadow?

_____

_____

_____

_____

Activity 2: Protecting yourself from the Sun's UV light

This child is playing on a beach. Draw as many objects as you can to protect the child from UV light from the Sun.

Choose one of the ways you can protect yourself from the Sun. Write a sentence to explain how it helps to keep you safe.

_____

_____

_____

_____

_____

Activity 3: Is your shadow always the same?

Make another shadow in the playground on a sunny afternoon. Think about what your shadow looked like in the morning and in the afternoon. How is your shadow similar to you, and how is it different from you?

Things to think about:

shadow size   colour of the shadow   shadow shape

how the shadow moves   any features of the shadow

Record your answers in the table.

Things about my shadow that are similar to me	Things about my shadow that are different from me

Key learning

In this lesson I have learnt that: **Shadows** are the same shape as the objects that cast them, but their size and position can change when the Sun (or other light source) moves. Your shadow is the same shape as you and moves with you, but has no features or detail.

As well as giving out light, the Sun gives out **ultraviolet (UV) light**. UV light from the Sun can be dangerous to your skin and eyes. **Opaque** objects, which block the **sunlight**, or materials that are good at reflecting sunlight can be used to protect your body from the Sun.

Homework

Look at home or in shops for products that protect us from UV light from the Sun. Add any that you didn't think of to your diagram. Some of these products will have an SPF number. Find out what this means.

Key vocabulary

light source   shadow

Activity 1: How does changing the height of the torch change the size of the shadow?

Explore making shadows with a torch. Find out what happens when you change the height of the torch. Answer the question below.

How did you make the shadow longer or shorter?

_____

_____

Complete the sentence.

The _____ the light source, the _____ the shadow.

You will need

- torch
- cup or other object

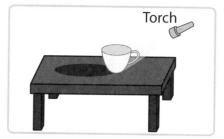

Torch

Activity 2: How can you change the size of the shadow on a screen?

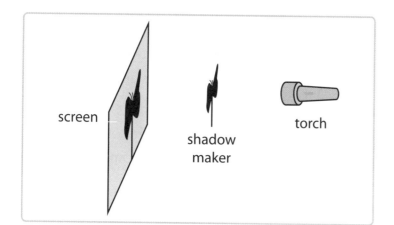

screen

shadow maker

torch

You will need

- screen
- torch
- card
- scissors
- sticky tape
- pencil/stick

Investigate how to change the size of a shadow on a screen.

Use the card and pencil or stick to create a shadow maker with an interesting shape. Make a shadow with the torch, shadow maker and screen. Explore making different shadows following the instructions in the table on the next page.

Draw the shadow in the first position.	Move the torch **closer to the shadow maker.** Keep the shadow maker and screen in the same place. Draw/write what happens to the shadow.	Move the torch **further away from the shadow maker.** Keep the shadow maker and screen in the same place. Draw/write what happens to the shadow.

What did you find out?

_____

_____

Complete the sentence to describe the pattern you found.

The _____ the torch is to the shadow maker the _____ the shadow is.

Key learning

In this lesson I have learnt that: Changing the position of the **light source** to be higher above the object, moving it further away or moving it to shine from a different direction can all change the size and position of an object's **shadow**. The closer the light source is to an object, the larger its shadow.

Homework

Some young children are afraid of their shadows. This is because they can appear alive, as they change in shape and size, and follow you around. Write a note to a younger child telling them why they should not be afraid of their shadow.

Friction and magnets

Lesson 1 **What makes it move?**

Key vocabulary

contact force   force   push   pull

Activity 1: What makes it move?

A **force** is a push or pull that can make something move or change shape.

When the object providing the force is touching the object that is moving, we call it a contact force.

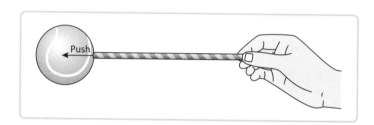

Look at the diagram above right. The straw is in contact with the ball when it is pushing it. This contact force makes the ball move.

Look at the pictures on the next page and write the objects that start to move. Was the force a push or a pull?

Object	Push? (✓)	Pull? (✓)

Activity 2: How can you move the ball?

Investigate different ways that you can move a ball.

Use different object(s) to move a ball in different ways. Can you move it in different ways?

Draw four diagrams to show the different ways you made the ball move.

Add arrows to show the direction the ball moved and label it with the word 'push' or 'pull'.

You will need

- table tennis ball
- lolly stick
- piece of adhesive tack
- piece of string
- paper fan
- small battery powered fan

<table>
<tr><td></td><td></td></tr>
<tr><td></td><td></td></tr>
</table>

Choose one way you moved the ball.

Write a sentence explaining how you moved the ball. Use the term 'contact force'.

_____

_____

Key learning

In this lesson I have learnt that: A **force** is a **push** or **pull** that can make something move or change shape. When the object providing the force is touching the object that is moving, we call it a **contact force**. A contact force could be a push or a pull.

Homework

Make a list of things you can move at home using a push or a pull. Explain to someone why this is called a contact force.

Key vocabulary

contact force   material   rough   smooth

Activity 1: How long does a spinning top spin on different surfaces?

A contact force is used to make a spinning top spin.

Your fingers are in contact with the spinning top when they push it to start it turning.

Investigate how long a spinning top can spin.

Spin your spinning top on five different surfaces made of different materials such as the carpet or a tabletop.

Measure the time it takes to stop spinning.

Write how you will do this investigation.

_____

_____

_____

You will need

- spinning top
- stopwatch
- five different surfaces made of different materials

Record your results in the table.

Surface	Time (in seconds)

Activity 2: What did you find out?

Rank the surfaces in order of how long it took the spinning top to stop. Write them next to the arrow.

Fastest

_____

_____

_____

_____

_____

Slowest

Complete the sentences.

The spinning top stops more quickly on a rough surface such as _____ because

_____ .

The spinning top spins for longer on a smooth surface such as _____ because

_____ .

The spinning top spins for longer on a _____ surface than on a _____ surface

because _____ .

The spinning top spins for about the same amount of time on surfaces such as _____ and

_____ because _____ .

Key learning

In this lesson I have learnt that: A **contact force** is used to make a spinning top spin. Your fingers are in contact with the spinning top when they push it to start it turning. The surface on which a spinning top is moving affects how long it spins for. Some surfaces are **rough**, others are **smooth**. The spinning top stops more quickly on a rough surface as the bumps make it harder to move.

Homework

Repeat the enquiry activity at home using a coin instead of a spinning top. Did you find a similar pattern?

Key vocabulary

material   rough   smooth

Activity 1: How well can an object slide on different surfaces?

Different surfaces are made of different materials. Some surfaces are **rough**, others are smooth. The type of surface can make it easier or harder for an object to move.

Investigate how well an object can slide on different materials.

Place an object on the ramp. Predict how high you will need to raise the ramp to make the object slide and write it in the table.

Raise the ramp until the object slides down it. Measure the height.

Change the material on the ramp and repeat.

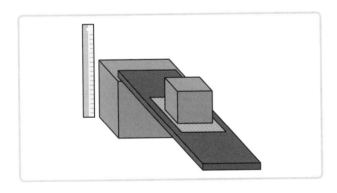

You will need

- block and plank to create a ramp
- object/plastic box
- materials to cover ramps (such as felt, foam, fabric, sandpaper, tin foil, plastic, carpet, rubber matting)

Record your predictions and results in the table.

Material	Prediction	Height lifted (in cm)

Activity 2: What did you find out?

Rank the materials in order of how easily (lowest height needed) the object slid down the ramp. Write them between the arrows, then complete the sentences below.

Lowest height _____ Slides most easily

_____

_____

_____

_____

Highest height _____ Slides least easily

The object slid more easily on a smooth surface such as _____ because

_____ .

The object did not slide as easily on a rough surface such as _____ because

_____ .

The object slides more easily on a _____ surface than on a _____ surface

because _____ .

The object slides about the same on surfaces such as _____ and _____

because _____ .

Key learning

In this lesson I have learnt that: Different surfaces are made of different **materials**. The type of surface can make it easier or harder for an object to move. An object slides more easily on **smooth** surfaces as there are fewer bumps to stop it moving.

Homework

At home or in the park, safely test how slippery different surfaces are to walk on. Which was the most slippery? Which was the least slippery? Talk with your parents/carers and do this activity with them to make sure you are safe.

Key vocabulary

attract	magnet	south pole
like poles	north pole	repel

Activity 1: What happens when you move different poles of a bar magnet together?

You will need

You will need

- 2 bar magnets

Investigate what happens when you move different poles of a bar magnet together.

Move the magnets together, as in each of the diagrams below. Discuss with a partner what happens each time.

Add arrows, like in the first diagram, to the second and third diagrams to show if they pull together or push apart.

Write the term 'attract' or 'repel' above the arrows in each diagram to describe what happened.

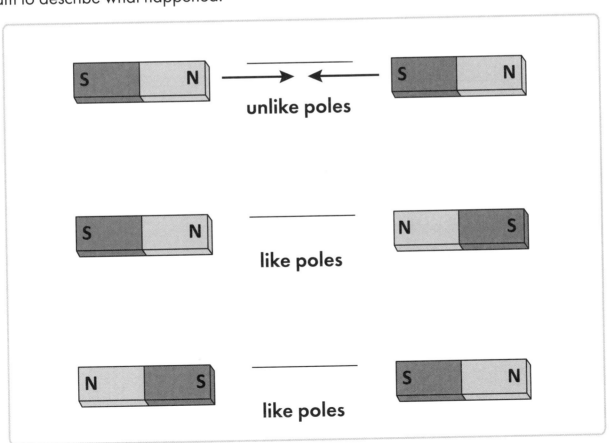

S   N   →   ←   S   N

unlike poles

S   N   _____   N   S

like poles

N   S   _____   S   N

like poles

Activity 2: What happens when you move different poles of a bar magnet and a horseshoe magnet together?

Move the magnets together in different ways so that different poles come together. What happens?

Draw two diagrams to show what you found out.

Add arrows to show whether they pull together, or push apart.

Then add the term 'attract' or 'repel' above the arrows to describe what happened.

Write how magnets affect one another below.

Use these key terms in your answer.

attract   **like poles**   **magnet**   **north pole**   **south pole**   **repel**

_____

_____

_____

Key learning

In this lesson I have learnt that: **Magnets** can be different shapes and sizes, but all magnets have two poles – a **south pole** (S on the magnet) and a **north pole** (N on the magnet).

If you bring **like poles** together (a north pole and a north pole or a south pole and a south pole), the two magnets will **repel** (push apart). If you bring unlike poles together (a north pole and a south pole), the two magnets will **attract** (pull towards one another).

Homework

Look for magnets in your home. What are they used for?

Key vocabulary

attract   magnetic   material   repel

Activity 1: Attract or repel?

Look at each diagram carefully, then draw a ring around the correct word, 'attract' or 'repel'.

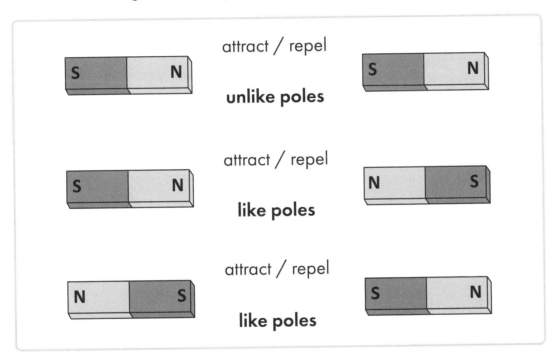

attract / repel

unlike poles

attract / repel

like poles

attract / repel

like poles

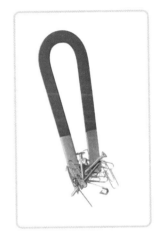

Draw a ring around the correct word to complete each of these sentences:

When two like / unlike poles are brought together they attract each other.

When two like / unlike poles are brought together they repel each other.

Activity 2: Which materials are magnetic?

Investigate which materials are magnetic. You know if a material is magnetic because it will be attracted to the magnet.

Record the name of each object and the material it is made from in the table on the next page, then use a magnet to find out if the material is magnetic.

You will need

- magnet
- objects to test (such as paperclips, coins, cans, keys, cutlery, marbles, beads, cubes)

Record your results in the table.

Name of object	Material	Magnetic or not?

Activity 3: What did you find out?

What type of scientific enquiry did you carry out to answer today's question?

_____

Which materials are magnetic?

_____

Which materials are not magnetic?

_____

Are all metals magnetic? How do you know?

_____

_____

Key learning

In this lesson I have learnt that: Some **materials** are **magnetic**. Magnetic materials are **attracted** to a magnet. Not all metals are magnetic.

Homework

Use a magnet to identify which metal objects in your house are magnetic, and which are not magnetic.

Key vocabulary

force   magnetic   material   non-contact force

Activity 1: Non-contact forces

Investigate the strength of a magnet by observing how well it attracts different magnetic materials.

Test the strength of your magnet using different methods. Use a method that shows that a magnetic force is a non-contact force. Draw a diagram to show your results.

You will need

- magnet
- ruler
- paperclips
- magnetic objects of different weights (such as a key, cutlery, cans)
- paper
- measuring scales

Activity 2: How strong are magnets?

In groups, test the strength of six different magnets.

How is your group going to test the strength of the magnets?

_____

_____

_____

_____

You will need

- 6 different sized magnets
- ruler
- paperclips
- a range of magnetic objects of different weights (such as keys, cutlery, scissors, cans, tins)
- paper
- measuring scales

Record your results in the table, then rank your magnets from strongest to weakest.

Magnet	
A	
B	
C	
D	
E	
F	

_____

_____

_____

_____

_____

_____

Which was the strongest magnet? How did you know?

_____

_____

_____

Activity 3: What did you find out?

Think about the class results and your own results.

Which of the statements in the speech bubbles is true?

_____

_____

_____

Key learning

In this lesson I have learnt that: Magnetic **materials** are attracted to a magnet. A **magnetic force** is a **non-contact force**, it does not need to touch the object it acts on. Non-contact forces act at a distance.

Homework

Find some magnets at home. Which is the strongest? How do you know?

Movement and nutrition for the human body

Lesson 1   What nutrients do we get from our food?

Key vocabulary

carbohydrate	energy	fibre	nutrient	sugar
diet	fat	minerals	protein	vitamin

Activity 1: Which foods give us which nutrients?

List some examples of foods that contain each of the different nutrients.

Nutrient	Examples of food
Carbohydrates	
Protein	
Healthy fats	
Fibre	
Vitamins	

Activity 2: What nutrients have you eaten?

Think about the food you have eaten today or you ate last night.

Choose one of the foods you have eaten. What type of food was it?

_____

What nutrients does it contain?

_____

How do these nutrients help your body?

_____

_____

Why is it important to eat a balance of different foods in your **diet**?

_____

_____

Key learning

In this lesson I have learnt that: Different types of food contain different **nutrients**. These are useful for our bodies in different ways. There are five main groups of nutrients:

1. **Carbohydrates** provide us with **energy** to move and keep warm. **Sugar** is a type of carbohydrate. It can give us a burst of energy.

2. **Proteins** are needed for growth.

3. **Fats** also provide us with energy and help to keep us warm.

4. **Fibre** (roughage) keeps our digestive system healthy and helps us go to the toilet regularly.

5. **Vitamins** and **minerals** keep us healthy and prevent us getting ill.

Homework

Draw your favourite meal, including a drink. Label all the parts of your meal with the food group to which each part belongs, and the nutrients it contains. How will your meal help your body? Is your meal missing any nutrients?

Key vocabulary

balanced   carbohydrate   diet   fat   fibre

minerals   nutrients   protein   vitamins

Activity 1: Which nutrients do school meals contain?

Look at the menu for a week. Either use the menu given below or use your school menu.

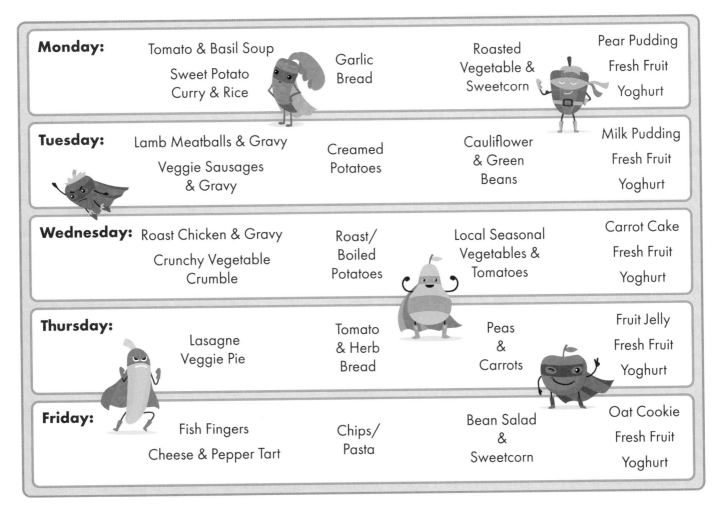

Monday:	Tomato & Basil Soup / Sweet Potato Curry & Rice	Garlic Bread	Roasted Vegetable & Sweetcorn	Pear Pudding / Fresh Fruit / Yoghurt
Tuesday:	Lamb Meatballs & Gravy / Veggie Sausages & Gravy	Creamed Potatoes	Cauliflower & Green Beans	Milk Pudding / Fresh Fruit / Yoghurt
Wednesday:	Roast Chicken & Gravy / Crunchy Vegetable Crumble	Roast/ Boiled Potatoes	Local Seasonal Vegetables & Tomatoes	Carrot Cake / Fresh Fruit / Yoghurt
Thursday:	Lasagne Veggie Pie	Tomato & Herb Bread	Peas & Carrots	Fruit Jelly / Fresh Fruit / Yoghurt
Friday:	Fish Fingers / Cheese & Pepper Tart	Chips/ Pasta	Bean Salad & Sweetcorn	Oat Cookie / Fresh Fruit / Yoghurt

Choose a colour for each nutrient. Add it to the key below:

Carbohydrates	Fats	Protein	Fibre	Vitamins and minerals

Use the colours to identify the different sources of nutrients in the menu. Circle each dish with the colour of the nutrient it contains. Many dishes will contain more than one nutrient.

Activity 2: Which foods give us which nutrients?

Complete the tally chart to check how many times each nutrient is eaten, and if they are eaten every day.

	Carbohydrates	Fats	Protein	Fibre	Vitamins and minerals
Monday					
Tuesday					
Wednesday					
Thursday					
Friday					

What did you find out? Are the school midday meals balanced? How do you know?

_____

_____

_____

Which is your favourite source of protein to eat? _____

Which way do you like to get your Vitamin C? _____

_____

Key learning

In this lesson I have learnt that: Different foods contain different **nutrients**. These include **carbohydrates, fats, proteins, fibre, vitamins** and **minerals**. It is important to eat a **balanced diet** to make sure you have all the nutrients to stay healthy.

Homework

Choose one of the nutrients you have learnt about. Design a 'Super-Nutrient' superhero to promote good health and explain how that nutrient helps the body stay healthy.

Key vocabulary

ribs   skeleton   spine
skull   spinal cord   x-ray

Activity 1: What bones make up the skeleton?

Label the diagram of the skeleton below. Use the words below to help.

ribs   pelvis   femur   skull   backbone   kneecap

Do you know the names of any other bones? Add these to your diagram.

Activity 2: What do the bones protect?

Match the bone to the vital organ it protects.

skull ● ● heart and lungs

spine ● ● brain

ribs ● ● spinal cord

As well as protecting your vital organs, what else does your skeleton do?

_____

Activity 3: What bones are these?

Look at these **x-rays**. Can you name the bones being shown?

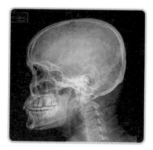 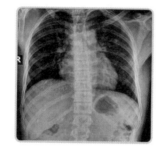 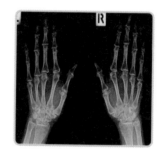

_____   _____   _____

Key learning

In this lesson I have learnt that: Your **skeleton** is made up of lots of bones. The skeleton has three important roles:

- to protect vital organs such as your brain
- to allow you to move
- for support – the bones in your legs, back and neck keep you upright.

Homework

Find out about what safety equipment you can wear when you are doing different sports to protect your bones. Draw a poster to explain when these should be worn, and why.

Key vocabulary

joint   muscle   skeleton   tendon

Activity 1: Where did you feel it?

Carry out the circuit training set out by your teacher. As you complete each station of the circuit training, mark where you felt the muscle working and label it with the correct activity number.

You will need

• small weights

1. biceps
2. triceps
3. abdominals
4. obliques
5. gluteals
6. quadriceps
7. calves

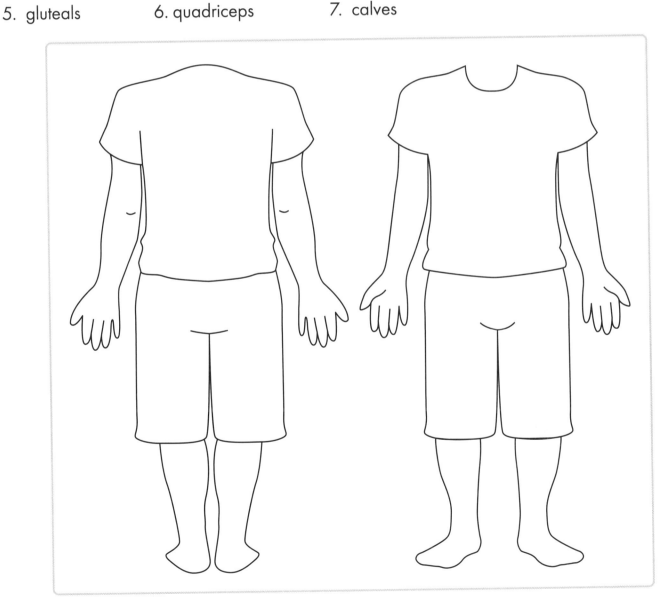

Activity 2: What did you find out?

Label the diagram below using the following key terms:

bone   **tendon**   **muscle**   **joint**

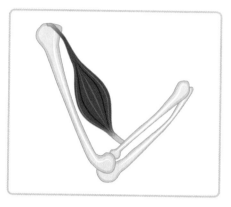

Use the diagram to explain how muscles help humans to move.

_____

_____

_____

What scientific skills have you used to find out and record how muscles help us move?

_____

_____

The diagram above shows an elbow joint. Can you name some other **joints**?

_____

Key learning

In this lesson I have learnt that: Our **muscles** are attached to our **skeleton** by **tendons**. The muscles pull on bones, which then make our bodies move. Different muscles move different parts of our bodies.

Homework

Find out about the joints in your legs from your pelvis to toes – your hip, knee, ankle and toes. What type of movement occurs at each joint?

Key vocabulary

exoskeleton   fluid   invertebrate   vertebrate

Activity 1: Which animals have an internal bony skeleton?

Circle the vertebrate animals.

woodlouse

penguin

snake

earthworm

elephant

fish

eel

ladybird

octopus

monkey

Write down two examples of invertebrates that are filled with fluid for support.

_____   _____

How do these animals move?

_____

_____

Write down two examples of invertebrates that have an exoskeleton.

_____   _____

How do these animals move?

_____

_____

Activity 2: What would it be like to have an exoskeleton?

Imagine you have an exoskeleton.

Talk with your partner. What would be good about having an exoskeleton? What would be bad?

Write into the table any positives, negatives and interesting points you have discussed.

Positive	Negative	Interesting

Key learning

In this lesson I have learnt that: **Vertebrate** bodies are supported by an internal bony skeleton. **Invertebrates** have no bony skeleton. Some invertebrates have a hard outer **exoskeleton** to provide protection and support. Other invertebrates contain lots of **fluid** to support their bodies.

Homework

Find out about an invertebrate animal. What kind of skeleton does this animal have? How does it move?

Key vocabulary

cartilage spine skull
ribs skeleton vertebrate

Activity 1: Which vertebrate does each skeleton belong to?

Name the animal each skeleton belongs to. Choose from:

fish **whale** **dog** **crocodile** **pigeon** **frog**

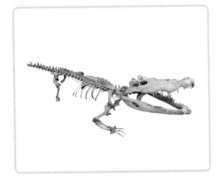

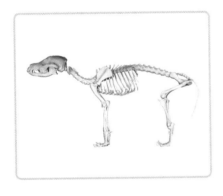

Activity 2: Observing vertebrate skeletons

Choose one of the skeletons above to observe carefully with a partner.

Fill in the table on the next page describing each of the main bones shown.

Share your findings with other pairs (who have studied different skeletons) and add them to your table. The first row has been done for you.

Animal	Skull	Spine	Ribs	Legs
Crocodile	long and pointy lots of teeth	long	six pairs	four short legs
Frog				
Dog				
Pigeon				
Fish				
Whale				

Activity 3: How are human skeletons different to other vertebrates?

List three differences between the animal skeletons you looked at and the human skeleton.

1. _____

2. _____

3. _____

Key learning

In this lesson I have learnt that: Humans are **vertebrates**. Like all vertebrates they have an internal **skeleton**. However, vertebrate skeletons do not all look the same. For example, they look different as animals move in different ways.

Homework

Choose a vertebrate. Print or draw a picture of their skeleton and label as many bones as you can. How is the skeleton different to a human skeleton?

Flowering plants and plant growth

Lesson 1   What do leaves do?

Key vocabulary

capture   comparative test enquiry   flower   leaf   roots   stem

Activity 1: What would happen if a plant lost its leaves?

Plan a **comparative test enquiry** to find out what would happen if a plant lost some or all of its leaves.

Answer the questions below to plan your enquiry.

What will you change about the plants?

_____

_____

What will you keep the same and how will you do this?

_____

_____

_____

What do you think will happen?

_____

_____

How will you measure or observe any changes?

_____

_____

How often will you make your measurements or observations?

_____

_____

You will need

- 3 potted plants
- labels
- digital camera (optional)
- rulers (optional)
- string (optional)

Activity 2: Record your observations

Observe your plants on three different days.

Use the boxes below to draw pictures and write any notes about your observations.

You may wish to measure and record the height of the plants at each observation. Do this by cutting string that is the same height of the plant and then measuring the string.

Observation 1   Date: _____

Plant 1 – all leaves	**Plant 2 – some leaves**	**Plant 3 – no leaves**

Observation 2   Date: _____

Plant 1 – all leaves	**Plant 2 – some leaves**	**Plant 3 – no leaves**

Observation 3   Date: _____

Plant 1 – all leaves	Plant 2 – some leaves	Plant 3 – no leaves

_____   _____   _____

_____   _____   _____

_____   _____   _____

Activity 3: What did you find out from your enquiry?

What did you observe about each plant? _____

_____

What does this tell you about why plants need leaves? Use the words 'light', 'leaf'/'leaves' and 'grow'/'growth' in your answer.

_____

_____

Key learning

In this lesson I have learnt that: All plants have **roots**, **stems** and **leaves**. Many plants also have **flowers**. Leaves **capture** sunlight. The plant uses energy from sunlight to produce food. Some of this food is used to make the plant grow. By removing some of the leaves, the amount of sunlight the plant can capture is decreased. Without any leaves, the plant cannot grow and will die.

Homework

Stand under a tree and look up at the leaves. Describe the arrangement of the leaves. Do the leaves overlap? Why do you think they are arranged in this way?

Key vocabulary

absorb	enquiry	observing over time	stem
anchor	nutrient	roots	transport

Activity 1: What do roots do?

You will carry out a comparative test enquiry to observe the roots on two different plants.

Draw and label the plants, showing any differences you have observed.

You will need

- two flowering plants of the same type (one with and one without roots)

plant with roots

plant with no roots

Use your observations to answer the question below.

What have you learnt from this enquiry?

_____

_____

_____

What does this enquiry tell you about what roots do?

_____

_____

_____

Activity 2: How is water transported around the plant?

You will set up an **observing over time enquiry** to find out how water is transported around the plant.

Draw and label how you have set up your enquiry below.

You will need
- celery stalk
- carnation
- beaker
- dye

Date: _____

What do you predict will happen to the celery and carnation?

_____

_____

_____

Activity 3: Results

Observe your celery and carnation after they have been left in the dye for a week. Cut the stems and draw what you see on the next page. Draw the flowers and add labels to explain what happened.

Date: _____

You will need

- celery stalk
- carnation
- cutting boards
- blunt household knives
- magnifier

Use your observations to answer the questions below.

What have you learnt from this enquiry? _____

_____

What are the functions of the root of a plant? _____

_____

What are the functions of the stem of a plant? _____

_____

Key learning

In this lesson I have learnt that: **Roots anchor** the plant into the soil. Roots **absorb nutrients** such as water and minerals from the soil. This water is **transported** to the leaves and flowers via small tubes in the **stem**. The stem also provides support for the plant and holds the leaves and flowers up.

Homework

When you are walking home or playing outside, look for evidence of tree roots. What do you notice about them? Can you see the roots of most plants?

Key vocabulary

capture/capturing   consumer   leaf   producer   roots   stem

Activity 1: Do plants need air?

Set up a comparative test enquiry to find out if plants need air.

Draw and label how you set up the enquiry.

Date: _____

You will need

- two healthy plants, both watered, one covered in a transparent plastic bag, secured with a rubber band

plant 1	**plant 2**

What do you predict will happen to the plants?

_____

_____

_____

Activity 2: Results

Draw and label the plants after a week, showing any differences you have observed. Write any notes below the pictures.

Date: _____

plant 1	**plant 2**

_____   _____

_____   _____

_____   _____

Use your observations to answer the questions below.

What have you learnt from this enquiry?

Use the words 'air', 'leaf'/'leaves', 'food' and 'grow'/'growth' in your answer.

_____

_____

What type of enquiry did you use to gather evidence to answer today's question?

_____

How do you know that it is that type of enquiry?

_____

_____

Activity 3: Graphic organiser: Flowering plant

Look at the picture of the plant.

Use the frame below to write down what you know about it.

Parts of the plant			
Roots	Stems	Leaves	Flowers
What would happen if the plant part was missing?			

Key learning

In this lesson I have learnt that: **Leaves** have tiny little holes in them which allow air into the plant. The energy **captured** from sunlight is used to turn air and water into the plant's food. Without air, a plant will not be able to produce food and will die. Plants are **producers** because they make their own food. Animals are **consumers** because they have to eat food.

Homework

Look at some plants that are growing indoors. Which way are the leaves facing? Why do you think this is? Is this the same for all the plants you have looked at?

Key vocabulary

nutrient   seed   sunlight

Activity 1: What happens if plants do not have enough space?

Set up a comparative test enquiry to find out what happens if plants do not have enough space.

Plant the seeds in the pots. Place lots of seeds close together in one pot. Place the seeds far apart in the other pot. Draw the two pots (viewed from above) to show how you have planted the **seeds**.

Date: _____

You will need
- seeds
- two pots
- soil

pot 1   pot 2

What do you predict will happen to the seeds?

_____

_____

_____

Activity 2: Results

Draw and label what your pots look like after two to three weeks.

Date: _____

pot 1

pot 2

_____   _____

_____   _____

_____   _____

Use your observations to answer the questions below.

What have you learnt from this enquiry?

Use the words 'water', 'light', 'nutrients' and 'grow'/'growth' in your answer.

_____

_____

What type of enquiry did you use to gather evidence to answer today's question?

_____

How do you know that it is that type of enquiry?

_____

_____

Activity 3: What do you predict will happen to the plants?

Write an answer to the following questions. How well do you think the cress plants in the picture will grow?

Why do you think that?

Use as many of the following words as you can in your answer.

roots	sunlight	stem
leaves	water	food
absorb	nutrients	space
compete	grow	

_____

_____

_____

_____

_____

_____

_____

Key learning

In this lesson I have learnt that: When plants do not have enough or much space to grow, we say they are overcrowded. Overcrowded plants compete with each other for **sunlight**, water and **nutrients**. Plants that are not able to have enough of what they need to produce their own food will not survive. Plants that are able to get more sunlight, water and nutrients will grow faster and bigger than the others.

Homework

Design your own seed packet. On the front draw the plants your seeds will grow into. On the back tell the gardener how to best plant the seeds, to make sure the plants grow as well as possible.

Key vocabulary

adaptation   adapted   habitat

Activity 1: How is the cactus suited to its habitat?

Look at the diagram of a cactus.

Think about how the stems, roots and leaves of the cactus are different to other plants you have studied.

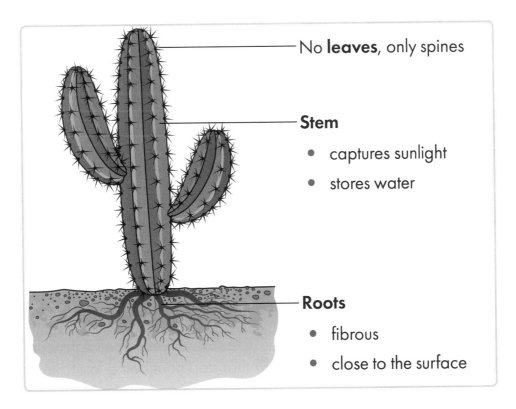

No **leaves**, only spines

Stem
- captures sunlight
- stores water

Roots
- fibrous
- close to the surface

Complete the sentences. Choose from these words.

desert   arctic   thick   thin   stem   store water   food

The cactus is adapted to live in _____ conditions because it has a _____

_____ . This means that it can _____ .

Write about another adaptation that the cactus has.

_____

_____

Activity 2: How is the plant adapted?

Use your own research and the information below to write the name of each plant under its photo.

liana vine   **dodder plant**   **cushion plant**   **pitcher plant**

Draw a line to match the plant to its adaptations.

Plant	Adaptations
 _____	Thin, flexible stem. Not strong enough to hold the plant upright, so grows around trees.
	Attaches itself to trees using thorns, spikes or 'glue'.
	The plant can climb up high before producing leaves where sunlight can reach them.
 _____	Does not have roots, so cannot absorb water and nutrients.
	Has very small leaves that cannot absorb sunlight to make food.
	Has thin, stringy stems that grow around other plants and pierce their stems to absorb their food, nutrients and water.
 _____	Short stems. Plant lies flat on the ground to stop it being blown away.
	Has lots of very small tightly packed leaves that stop heat being lost from the soil, so keeps the plant warmer.
	Deep, long roots to absorb any water and nutrients.
 _____	Specially shaped leaves traps insects, which are attracted to the plants by their colour and smell.
	Liquid in the trap digests the insect's body and provides the plant with nutrients.
	Has other leaves that make food using air, water and energy from sunlight.

Design your own adapted plant. Where does it live? How is it adapted? Draw and label your plant below.

Key learning

In this lesson I have learnt that: Different plants live in different **habitats**. These habitats provide plants with different amounts of light, water, nutrients and room to grow. Some plants can live in hot conditions, while others can live in cold ones. Some live where there is a lot of water, and some can live where there is very little. That is why not all plants are the same. Plants have special **adaptations** (features) which help them to grow in a specific habitat; they are **adapted** to live there. This means that they may have different-shaped stems, leaves or roots, which may have different functions.

Homework

Find out about a plant that lives in extreme conditions such as in the Arctic or the desert. Draw a picture of the plant and label its adaptations for surviving in this habitat.

Module 6

Flowering plants life cycle

Lesson 1   What is inside a flower?

Key vocabulary

carpel	ovule	pollen	stamen
ovary	petal	sepal	

Activity 1: Flowering plant life cycle

This activity revisits what you learnt in Year 2 about the life cycle of flowering plants.

Label the main stages in the life cycle of a flowering plant.

seed   seedling   germinates   grows   makes seeds   mature plant

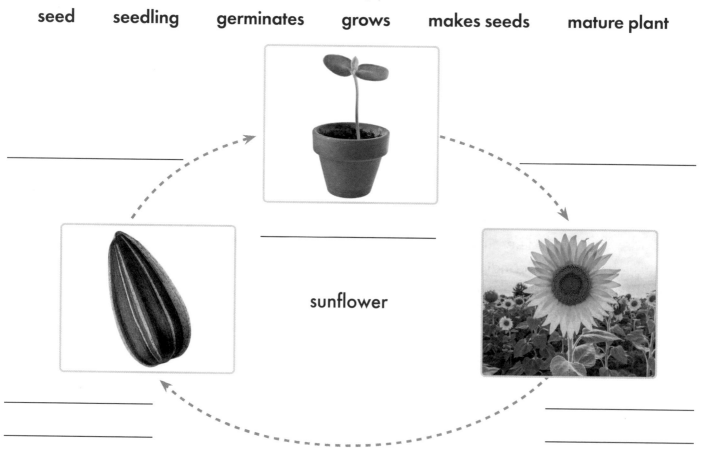

sunflower

_____

Which part of a plant do you think makes the seeds? _____

Activity 2: Parts of a flower

Read the information below and label the parts of the flower in the picture.

The flower produces the plant's seeds. A flower has a female part, called the carpel. This includes the ovary, which contains ovules. It has male parts, called stamens, that produce pollen. Petals surround the male and female parts, and sepals cover the flower when it is in bud.

petal   **sepal**   **stamen (male part)**   **carpel (female part)**   **ovary**

The male part of the plant produces pollen. Draw and label some pollen on your flower.

The female part of the plant produces ovules. Add some small circles to your flower and label them ovules.

Use the diagram and the information about flowers to answer the questions.

Which part of a flower is brightly coloured? _____

What do the sepals do?

_____

_____

Activity 3: Dissecting a flower

Dissect a flower into its individual parts.

Record your observations in the grid below. Draw one of each flower part.

You will need

- flower
- magnifier
- knife
- chopping board

Sepal	Petal
Carpel	Stamen

Key learning

In this lesson I have learnt that: The flower produces the plant's seeds. A flower has:

- a female part, called the **carpel**. This includes the **ovary**, which contains **ovules**
- male parts, called **stamens** which produce **pollen**
- **petals** which surround the male and female parts
- **sepals** which cover the flower when it is in bud.

Homework

Look at two different flowers. These can be real, in a book or on a computer. Look carefully at the shape, colour and number of the sepals, petals, stamens and carpel. Write or draw what you have found out.

Key vocabulary

carpel	petal	pollination	stamen
nectar	pollen	pollinator	

Activity 1: Pollination

Look at the diagram below, then complete the sentence to describe what happens during pollination.

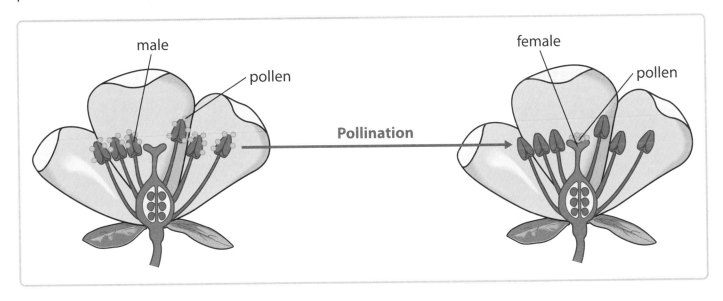

Pollination is when _____ from the _____ part of one flower, is transferred

to the _____ part of another flower.

Why might a pollinator visit a flower?

_____

_____

_____

_____

_____

_____

How does a flower attract a pollinator?

_____

_____

Can you name some animals that act as pollinators?

_____

_____

_____

_____

Activity 2: Pollination mime

Use the space below to plan a mime performance to show how insects transfer pollen from one plant to another.

How will you represent each of the following parts of a flower?

petals

_____

stamens

_____

carpel

_____

What will you use to represent the pollen? _____

Use the table on the next page to decide what will happen at each stage in your mime and what the narrator will say.

You will need

- props to represent pollen, e.g. pom poms
- cut-out discs of paper
- card

Stage	What is happening?	What will you or the narrator say?
1		
2		
3		
4		
5		

Key learning

In this lesson I have learnt that: **Pollen** is made by the **stamen**, the male part of the plant. **Pollination** is when the pollen from one flower is transferred to another flower. This needs to happen for seeds to be made. Animals that transfer pollen are called **pollinators**. Examples of pollinators are bees, birds, bats and butterflies.

Homework

The Rafflesia flower produces a scent that smells like rotting meat. Find out how it is pollinated.

Key vocabulary

carpel	ovule	pollen	stamen
ovary	petal	pollination	

Activity 1: A wind-pollinated flower

Pollination can occur by animals or the wind.

Label the parts of the wind-pollinated flower.

petal   sepal   stamen   carpel   ovary

Use the diagram and labels to answer the questions.

Where are the ovules made?

_____

Where is the pollen made?

_____

Where does the pollen land when it is transferred to another flower?

_____

Activity 2: Similarities and differences

Look at the structure of a wind-pollinated and an insect-pollinated flower.

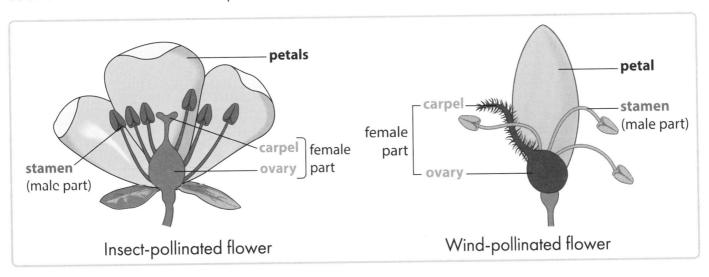

Insect-pollinated flower

Wind-pollinated flower

Use the diagrams above to answer the questions.

How are the two flowers similar?

_____

_____

How are the two flowers different?

_____

_____

Activity 3: Observing wind-pollinated flowers

You will need
- grass flower
- magnifier

Look carefully at a grass flower. What can you see?

Draw or write down your observations.

Activity 4: Wind-pollinated or insect-pollinated flower?

Complete the table. Match each statement below to a wind-pollinated flower or an insect-pollinated flower.

Give reasons for your choices.

Statement	Wind-pollinated flower? (✓)	Insect-pollinated flower? (✓)	Why?
I am brightly coloured.			
I am large.			
I have feathery female parts which hang outside of the flower.			
I do not produce nectar.			
I produce a scent.			
My male parts are hidden inside the petals.			
I produce lots of pollen.			

Activity 5: What type of flower?

Complete the table. Decide whether each flower is wind pollinated or insect pollinated.

Give reasons for your choices.

Flower	Wind or insect pollinated	Why?
tulip		
pussy willow		
oak		
lavender		

Which of the flowers do you think would produce nectar and / or a scent?

Key learning

In this lesson I have learnt that: **Pollination** can occur by animals or the wind. Insect-pollinated flowers are usually large and colourful and often produce a scent and nectar to attract a pollinator. The male and female parts are found between the **petals**. Wind-pollinated flowers are often very small, green and do not produce nectar or a scent. They produce lots of **pollen** and the male and female parts hang outside of the petals so the wind can carry the pollen from one flower to another.

Homework

Hay fever is caused by a reaction to the pollen produced by wind-pollinated flowers. Explain to hay fever sufferers you know why there is pollen in the air.

Lesson 4 — What are fruits?

Key vocabulary

fruit   ovary   pollination   seed

Activity 1: What is inside a fruit?

After a flower is pollinated, a fruit develops from the flower.

Safely, cut your fruit in half.

Record your observations by drawing the cut fruit.

Label your drawing using the terms:

ovary   **seed**   **stem**

> **You will need**
> - fruit
> - serrated knife
> - chopping board

Label where the fruit was attached to the rest of the flower.

Name some other fruits.

_____

_____

What do all fruits have inside them? _____

Are all fruits sweet? How do you know?

_____

_____

Activity 2: How fruits form

Describe what is happening to the tomato plant in each picture.

_____ _____ _____

_____ _____ _____

_____ _____ _____

_____ _____ _____

_____ _____ _____

_____ _____ _____

Key learning

In this lesson I have learnt that: After a flower is **pollinated**, a **fruit** develops from the flower. The **ovary** swells up (gets bigger) and becomes the fruit, and **seeds** form inside the ovary. All fruits contains seeds.

Homework

Write a letter to a supermarket manager explaining why some of their 'vegetables' should be in the fruit aisle.

Key vocabulary

dispersal   fruit   nutrient   pollination

Activity 1: How are these seeds dispersed?

Look at the photos of different plants. How do you think the seeds are dispersed?

mistletoe

coconut

alpine sea holly

willow herb

pea

tomato

dandelion

dog rose

acacia

blackberry

sycamore

Himalayan balsam

Decide which method of seed dispersal each plant from page 81 uses and record your findings in the table below. Give reasons why you put the plants in different groups.

Seed dispersal method	Examples	Why did you put it in this group?
attached to an animal		
using the wind		
being eaten by an animal and spread in their droppings		
by explosion of the seedpod (fruit)		
using water		

Activity 2: Seed dispersal model

Use junk modelling to design and make a fruit and seed that can be dispersed.

What seed dispersal mechanism is your group modelling?

_____

_____

Draw and label your model below to explain how the fruit and seed is dispersed.

You will need

junk modelling equipment, such as

- paper
- feathers
- cotton wool
- cardboard
- split pins
- plastic food pots
- dried peas
- string

Key learning

In this lesson I have learnt that: Seed **dispersal** is when seeds are moved away from the plant that produced them. They are moved away so they do not compete for space, sunlight, water and **nutrients**. Seeds are dispersed by wind, water, animals eating **fruit**, seeds becoming attached to an animal, and through explosions of a seedpod (fruit).

Homework

Find out how poppies disperse their seeds. Draw a cartoon strip showing how a poppy flower is **pollinated**, turns into a fruit and disperses its seeds.

William Collins' dream of knowledge for all began with the publication of his first book in 1819.
A self-educated mill worker, he not only enriched millions of lives, but also founded a flourishing publishing house. Today, staying true to this spirit, Collins books are packed with inspiration, innovation and practical expertise.
They place you at the centre of a world of possibility and give you exactly what you need to explore it.

Published by Collins
An imprint of HarperCollins*Publishers*
The News Building, 1 London Bridge Street, London, SE1 9GF, UK

HarperCollins*Publishers*
Macken House, 39/40 Mayor Street Upper, Dublin 1, D01 C9W8, Ireland

Browse the complete Collins catalogue at
collins.co.uk

ISBN 978-0-00-868324-5

British Library Cataloguing-in-Publication Data
A catalogue record for this publication is available from the British Library.

Development Editor: Jo Locke
Series Editor: Jane Turner
Consultant Reviewer: David Allen
Publisher: Laura White
Copyeditor: Kariss Holgarth
Proofreader: Sarah Snashall
Cover Designer: Amparo at Kneath Associates
Packager: Oriel Square
Typesetter: Tech-Set
Production Controller: Alhady Ali
Printed and bound in Great Britain by Martins the Printers

MIX
Paper | Supporting
responsible forestry
FSC™ C007454

This book contains FSC™ certified paper and other controlled
sources to ensure responsible forest management.

For more information visit: www.harpercollins.co.uk/green

collins.co.uk/sustainability

Acknowledgements
This work is adapted from the original work, Snap Science Second Edition Year 3.
All images are from Shutterstock.

The publishers gratefully acknowledge the permission granted to reproduce the copyright material in this book. Every effort has been made
to trace copyright holders and to obtain their permission for the use of copyright material. The publishers will gladly receive any information
enabling them to rectify any error or omission at the first opportunity.